Strategies for Trading in The Zone

A Psychological Edge for Unmatched Market Performance

Chinedu Brown

Trading in The Zone

Copyright© 2024 Chinedu Brown

All rights reserved

Trading in The Zone

Table of Contents

INTRODUCTION ---------- 6

The Psychological Edge of Trading ---------- 6
    Why Trading Psychology Matters ---------- 7
    How This Book Can Transform Your Trading ---------- 10

CHAPTER ONE ---------- 16

The Zone: What It Is and How to Reach It ---------- 16
    What is "The Zone" in Trading? ---------- 17
    Flow State and Trading Performance. ---------- 19
    Techniques for Entering the Zone. ---------- 20

CHAPTER TWO ---------- 26

The Path to Success: Trading with Mental Clarity. ---------- 26
    Three Foundations: Fundamental, Technical, and Mental Analysis. ---------- 28
    Why Mental Analysis Is Crucial to Mastery ---------- 30
    How Psychology Can Help You Stay "In the Zone" ---------- 32
    Balancing Technical Skills and Psychological Discipline. ---------- 33

CHAPTER THREE ---------- 36

The allure (and perils) of Trading ---------- 36
    The Excitement of Trading ---------- 37
    The Risks of Overconfidence and Greed ---------- 39
    The Emotional Rollercoaster ---------- 41
    The Thin Line Between Discipline and Impulsivity ---------- 43
    Finding Balance. ---------- 44

CHAPTER FOUR ---------- 46

Take Responsibility for Your Trades — 46
- Accountability in Trading: No Blame, Only Ownership — 47
- How Responsibility Contributes to Mental Control — 49
- Let Go of External Factors: News and Market Noise — 51
- Developing Self-Reliance: Trusting Your Trading Plan — 53

CHAPTER FIVE — 56

Consistency, the Ultimate Mental State. — 56
- Create a Consistent Trading Process — 57
- Consistency and Emotional Stability — 58
- The Function of Routine in Mental Strength — 60
- How to Develop a Consistent Trading Mindset — 62

CHAPTER SIX — 66

The Dynamics of Perception in Trading — 66
- How Perception Drives Decision-Making. — 67
- Detecting Biases and False Perceptions in Trading — 68
- Perception vs. Reality: What the Market Really Says. — 71
- Train Your Mind to See Opportunities Clearly — 72

CHAPTER SEVEN — 76

Understanding the Market's Perspective. — 76
- Understanding the Market Through the Lens of Collective Psychology — 77
- How Markets Respond to Human Emotions — 79
- Understanding Market Sentiment and Crowd Behavior. — 81
- Adapting Your Mindset to Market Trends — 84

CHAPTER EIGHT — 88

The Trader's Perspective: Examining Chances — 88
- Trading in the Zone: Probability-Based Thinking — 89
- Overcoming the Certainty Trap and Embracing Risk — 91
- How to Create a Probability-Based Trading Strategy — 93

Mental Exercises to Strengthen Probability Thinking ------------------------- 95

CHAPTER NINE --- 98

Managing Your Beliefs for Trading Success --------------------------------- 98
Identifying and Analyzing Core Beliefs for Trading ------------------------- 99
How Your Beliefs Influence Your Trading Behavior. ----------------------- 101
How to Change Limiting Beliefs to Gain a Psychological Advantage. ---- 103
Developing Positive Trading Beliefs for Long-Term Success -------------- 106

CHAPTER TEN -- 110

The Nature of Belief in Trading -- 110
Formation of Belief in the Mind -- 111
How Subconscious Beliefs Impact Trading Decisions ---------------------- 113
Beliefs and the Development of Confidence -------------------------------- 115
Changing Negative Beliefs for Better Performance ------------------------- 117

CHAPTER ELEVEN --- 122

The Effect of Beliefs on Trading Results ----------------------------------- 122
How Beliefs Can Improve or Disrupt Trading Results --------------------- 123
Examining Real-Life Case Studies of Trader Beliefs ----------------------- 125
Reframing Self-Limiting Beliefs as Empowering --------------------------- 128
Practical Ways to Rewire Beliefs for Success ------------------------------- 130

CHAPTER TWELVE -- 134

Think Like a Trader in the Zone. --- 134
Developing a "Zone" Mindset for Peak Performance. ----------------------- 135
How to Maintain Emotional Detachment from the Market ------------------ 136
Developing a Long-Term, Process-Oriented Mindset. ---------------------- 138
Continuous Growth: Maintaining a Sharp and Adaptable Mindset. -------- 140

CONCLUSION -- 146

The Ultimate Psychological Edge for Trading ---------------------------------146
    Key Lessons for Consistent, Zone-based Trading.----------------------------147
    The Way Forward: Mastering the Art of Trading in the Zone --------------150
    Final Thoughts on Trading Success---152

INTRODUCTION

The Psychological Edge of Trading

Trading in the financial markets may be both thrilling and mentally taxing. Many traders join the market with a thorough understanding of fundamental and technical research, but only a small percentage attain consistent success. Why is this happening? The answer lies in a lesser-known but crucial part of trading: psychology. Your mindset—how you think, feel, and respond—determines whether you win or fail at trading.

In this book, we will focus on developing this critical skill: staying "in the zone." The zone is a mental condition in which you make decisions that are clear, objective, and precise. It's where distractions disappear, and you can consistently implement your trading strategy, regardless of what the market throws at you. This state is not accidental; it is the outcome of developing a trading mindset based on mental discipline, self-awareness, and strategic thinking. This is your psychological advantage.

Why Trading Psychology Matters

Trading involves analyzing charts, reading news, and researching economic reports. While these tools are valuable, they are not the whole picture. Successful traders understand that their thinking is their most valuable asset—and, at times, their greatest challenge. Emotions such as fear, greed, overconfidence, and anxiety can cause traders to make rash judgments, disregard their strategy, or abandon a trade too early. These emotional responses are typically generated by a failure to control the psychological stresses associated with trading.

The reality is that markets are unpredictable. Even with the best analysis, you will encounter trades that do not go your way. How you handle these events defines you as a trader. Do you stay calm and composed, or do you panic and make snap decisions? Do you stick to your plans, or do emotions cloud your judgment? This is where psychology distinguishes top traders from everyone else.

Many beginners feel that improving their technical skills or learning additional market indicators will fix their troubles. However, no amount of technical knowledge can compensate for a lack of mental discipline. The traders who win have learned to control their emotions, think in probabilities, and remain disciplined under pressure.

Achieving Maximum Performance Through the "zone."

The concept of a zone is not limited to trading. It is frequently referenced in the field of athletic psychology. Athletes define being in the zone as the time when they feel unstoppable—when their focus is razor-sharp, and they perform at their peak without being distracted by pressure or the fear of failure. For traders, the zone is very similar. It is a mental state in which all actions are deliberate, intentional, and based on a strong sense of confidence and discipline.

However, getting into the zone and, more importantly, staying there is not an easy process. It takes self-awareness, mental training, and the ability to emotionally detach from your trades. This book is intended to help you create this mindset, allowing you to perform consistently even during the most unpredictable market conditions. When you trade in the zone, you don't react rashly to market fluctuations. Instead, you calmly observe, analyze, and execute your trades with precision.

How This Book Can Transform Your Trading

In this book, we will look at tactics that go beyond charts and data. We will look at the psychological components of trading, which are often disregarded but are critical to generating consistent outcomes. You'll learn how to improve your mental clarity, stay focused, and build emotional resilience so you can handle both successes and defeats gracefully.

The primary areas we'll discuss are:

- ***The Path to Mental Mastery:*** Understanding why mental analysis is equally vital as fundamental or technical analysis. You'll learn how to strike a balance between these three parts in order to develop a thorough trading strategy.

- ***Recognizing Emotional pitfalls:*** We'll look at the emotional pitfalls that traders fall into, such as overtrading, chasing losses, and allowing fear to keep them from taking profitable trades.

- ***Taking accountability:*** You'll learn the significance of accepting complete accountability for your trading decisions. This is an important step toward developing confidence and self-reliance as a trader.

- ***Building Consistency:*** Successful traders are known for their consistency. We'll show you how to create regular habits and a routine that keeps you in the zone day after day.

- ➢ ***The Power of Perception:*** You'll discover how to change your perception of the market by removing cognitive biases that distort your perspective and lead to poor decisions.

- ➢ ***Thinking in possibilities:*** We'll help you adjust your attitude from expecting certainty to accepting possibilities so you may approach the market with a clear understanding of risk and return.

- ➢ ***Understanding Views and Their Impact:*** Your views about trading have a direct impact on your performance. We'll help you identify and change any limiting thoughts that are holding you back.

➢ **_Developing the Trader's Mindset:_** Finally, we'll teach you how to think like a trader—calm, composed, and ready to respond to shifting market conditions.

The Road Ahead

This journey is about more than just learning new tactics; it's about changing your mindset and emotions about trading. Mastering the mental game of trading will need time, effort, and dedication to personal development. There will be times when the market tests your emotions and others when you feel dissatisfied or uncertain. However, gaining a psychological edge will provide you with the clarity and control required to successfully handle those hurdles.

The purpose of this book is to help you become a more confident, disciplined, and lucrative trader. By the conclusion, you'll have the tools and methods to stay in the zone, even in the most volatile markets. You'll be able to approach each trade with a calm, clear mind and execute your strategy without being swayed by other influences.

The zone is not a physical location but rather a mental state. And once you learn how to stay in that mindset, you'll be able to realize your trading career's full potential. Let us begin this transformative adventure together.

CHAPTER ONE

The Zone: What It Is and How to Reach It

Being "in the zone" is one of the most elusive yet powerful sensations a trader can experience. This term is used in a variety of fields, including athletics, creative activity, and even high-level business, but it has a special meaning in Trading. When you're in the zone, everything comes together. You make precise conclusions without hesitation or second-guessing. The charts appear crisper, your inputs and exits are more precise, and, most crucially, you are emotionally separated from the outcome of each trade. You seem to be one step ahead of the market. But what precisely is this enigmatic "zone," and how does one reach there?

What is "The Zone" in Trading?

In Trading, the zone is commonly referred to as a flow state—a psychological state in which you are completely engrossed in the work at hand, your talents are properly matched to the challenge, and everything appears to go smoothly. It's a mental state in which time fades away, distractions vanish, and you're entirely concentrated on carrying out your strategy. This level of attention enables traders to maintain a sense of calm and clarity, even in volatile markets.

The zone is more than just being focused; it's about striking a balance between confidence and humility. Traders in the zone believe in their strategy and their ability to execute it, but they also understand that the market is unpredictable. They are willing to change if necessary, without becoming overconfident or reckless.

I recall the first time I encountered the zone. It occurred during an especially tumultuous market session. The charts were moving quickly, and many traders I knew were panicked. However, I felt absolutely peaceful, as if I were viewing the market from a distance. Every movement I made felt effortless. I wasn't doubting myself or overanalyzing. I simply followed my strategy and let the market unfold. At the end of the day, I found I had made numerous consecutive profitable trades. That experience taught me that the zone is not a myth; it is a state that any trader can achieve with the correct mentality and strategy.

Flow State and Trading Performance.

Mihaly Csikszentmihalyi, a psychologist, coined the term "flow state" to characterize a mental state of complete immersion in an activity. In Trading, this flow state frequently results in peak performance. But accomplishing it needs more than simply skill; it necessitates striking the perfect balance between challenge and ability.

When the market delivers a task that is appropriate for your level of preparation and expertise, you are more likely to enter the zone. On the other hand, if the challenge is too easy, you risk becoming complacent. If it is too difficult, frustration and stress will take over, making it hard to achieve the flow state.

To improve trading performance, you must understand when you are nearing the flow state and when you are deviating from it. If you find yourself bored or overconfident, it may be time to reconsider your strategy. If you're stressed or frustrated, take a moment to restore your calm. The zone thrives when you discover the right balance of challenge and expertise, not when you're under pressure.

Techniques for Entering the Zone.

Achieving the zone is a process, and while you can't force it, you may use techniques to improve your odds of going there. The first and most important step is preparation. You cannot expect to enter the zone until you complete your homework. This includes knowing your trading strategy inside and out, understanding the markets in which you trade, and planning for all possible outcomes.

> ➤ ***Mastery of Your Strategy:*** To enter the zone, you must trust your system implicitly. This needs much back-testing, forward testing, and practice. The more comfortable you are with your strategy, the less you will have to think about it during live Trading, allowing your actions to become natural.

> ***Mental and Physical Readiness:*** Traders must prepare their thoughts and bodies in the same way as athletes do before a game. Your mental clarity and focus can be greatly enhanced by getting adequate sleep, eating healthfully, and staying hydrated. Meditation or breathing techniques before your trading session might also help you relax and focus.

> ***Minimizing Distractions:*** Because the zone requires entire focus, distractions must be eliminated. Make sure your trading environment promotes intense attention. Turn off any superfluous notifications, clean up your workplace, and schedule a trading session when you can be totally present.

> ***Emotional Control:*** Emotions can be a major impediment to entering the zone. Fear, greed, and frustration can knock you out of the flow state faster than any technical

problem. Emotional detachment from the results of each trade is a helpful practice. Concentrate on implementing your strategy and let the results take care of themselves.

➢ *Visualization:* This may seem weird, but visualization is an effective strategy for getting into the zone. Before you start trading, spend a little time envisioning how you want the day to go. Imagine yourself making calm and confident decisions while watching the market evolve without tension. Rehearsing these mental patterns increases your chances of executing them in real life.

➢ *Ritual and Ritual:* Establishing a pre-trading ritual can help your brain recognize that it is time to focus. This might be as simple as evaluating your strategy, practicing a little meditation, or monitoring critical market data. Over time, these simple routines develop indicators that make it easier to go into the zone.

It's okay if you don't always enter the zone when you trade. Build habits and behaviors that boost the likelihood of reaching that state. When you are in the zone, you are not just a better trader but also the best version of yourself. This is where actual trading success rests.

By learning the discipline, preparation, and emotional control required to reach the zone, you will position yourself for unrivaled market performance. The zone is where your psychological edge emerges, and with practice, it will become a natural part of your trading experience.

Trading in The Zone

CHAPTER TWO

The Path to Success: Trading with Mental Clarity.

Trading success is sometimes described as a combination of technical analysis and fundamental study, but this just scratches the surface. True mastery stems from mental clarity, an often-overlooked facet of trading that enables you to make decisions free of emotional influence. The most successful traders rely on more than just strategies and charts; they've developed the psychological fortitude required to survive under duress.

In my early trading days, I was overly focused on technical indicators, as do many newbies. I was riveted to my screens, examining patterns and

Trading in The Zone

attempting to forecast market movements with accuracy. While this provided me a good start, I soon understood that success was more than simply what I knew technically; it was also about how I behaved myself mentally. I would second-guess my trades, withdraw prematurely out of fear, or be hesitant to engage when the setup was evident due to previous losses.

My emotions were dictating my choices, and it was evident that I needed to regain control of my thoughts if I was to succeed.

Three Foundations: Fundamental, Technical, and Mental Analysis.

The world of trading is built around three pillars: fundamental analysis, technical analysis, and mental analysis. Many traders only focus on the first two, ignoring the third, which is frequently the deciding factor between success and failure.

- ➤ *Fundamental analysis* looks at the underlying elements that determine currency prices. It includes analyzing economic statistics, news events, and geopolitical happenings that influence market mood.

- ➤ *Technical analysis* identifies trading opportunities by examining charts, patterns, and historical data. Traders seek out trends, support, and resistance levels, as well as price patterns that indicate prospective market movements.

- ➤ *Mental Analysis* focuses on understanding your personal psychology, learning how to stay calm under pressure, and building the emotional resilience needed to deal with the market's ups and downs. Most traders fail to perform adequate mental analysis.

The issue emerges when traders rely too much on either fundamental or technical analysis, forgetting the crucial role of mental analysis. You can have the best strategies in the world, but if your emotions take precedence over rationality, they will be rendered ineffective.

Why Mental Analysis Is Crucial to Mastery

Mental analysis is the glue that keeps everything together in trading. It allows you to stick to your strategy, execute trades with confidence, and retain consistency over time. Even if you have a strong technical basis, you are likely to destroy your efforts unless you master the psychological aspects of trading.

One of my most distinct trading recollections involves a well-planned setup. Everything lined up—the technicals were flawless, and the fundamentals supported my conclusion. However, I hesitated. In that split second of uncertainty, the market shifted, and I missed my entry. A few minutes later, the trade would have gone exactly as planned, and I would have made a significant profit. Instead, I was left angry, not because the strategy was flawed, but because I allowed fear and hesitation to enter. This is the essence of mental clarity. Without it, even the finest plans can fail.

Mental analysis encourages you to trust your strategy and your capacity to implement it. It assists you in managing the natural emotions that come with trading—fear, greed, excitement, and frustration—so that they do not obscure your judgment. You learn to detach from the outcome of each trade and focus on the process, allowing the results to unfold organically.

How Psychology Can Help You Stay "In the Zone"

To have consistent success in trading, you must have the mental discipline to stay "in the zone." But what does that actually mean? Being in the zone is achieving a mental state of focus and flow in which you are fully involved in the job at hand. In trading, this involves being able to execute trades calmly and clearly, unaffected by emotional emotions.

Trading in The Zone

When you're in the zone, you don't doubt yourself or allow fear to influence your actions. You are confidently and precisely implementing your trading plan, staying present and focused on the current trade rather than stressing about the outcome or previous mistakes.

For example, I recall a period when I was on a winning streak—trade after trade was successful. As my confidence developed, I could feel myself becoming overconfident. That is a risky place to be in trading since it frequently leads to unwarranted risks. Staying in the zone necessitates ongoing self-awareness and the capacity to identify when your emotions, especially positive ones such as confidence, become out of control. It's important to maintain a healthy perspective regardless of what the market throws at you.

Balancing Technical Skills and Psychological Discipline.

Trading is more than just implementing a strategy; it's also about establishing the mental fortitude to stick to that strategy even when the market tests your will. Many traders suffer because they focus too much on developing their technical skills and ignore the psychological discipline required to succeed. They devote hours to scrutinizing charts and fine-tuning strategies, but they fail to grasp that the true struggle is conducted within their own minds.

The finest traders I know cannot foresee every market action with pinpoint accuracy. They're the ones who've learned to control their emotions, resist impulses, and maintain discipline in the face of uncertainty. They understand that trading is about risk management and following a process that is not always correct.

When you combine great technical skills with psychological discipline, you have a powerful formula for success. Technical analysis provides you with the tools you need to navigate the market, whereas mental analysis gives you the strength to use those skills effectively.

To summarize, knowledge of market fundamentals or technical indicators is not sufficient to achieve trading success. It needs the ability to maintain mental clarity and discipline in the midst of emotional ups and downs. Trading in the zone entails conquering your thoughts and cultivating a mindset that enables you to execute consistently, independent of external circumstances. By combining technical skills with psychological discipline, you can acquire the mental clarity required for long-term success.

CHAPTER THREE

The allure (and perils) of Trading

Trading holds an inherent charm. Every year, thousands of people are drawn to trading because of the promise of financial freedom, the potential for large returns in a short period of time, and the pure exhilaration of playing in the markets. The thought of being your own boss, working from anywhere in the world, and reaching success that allows for complete independence is quite appealing. I vividly recall the first time I heard about FX trading. My acquaintance was making trades, making great profits, and discussing how he had found the path to financial independence. I was immediately intrigued, and I soon got in, ready to feel the thrill of the markets for myself.

However, as I quickly discovered, the allure of trading comes with substantial risks. The same excitement that draws individuals to the markets can also be their undoing. If you don't approach trading with the appropriate mindset and discipline, it may quickly transform from a rewarding venture to a frustrating and financially draining one. This chapter focuses on understanding the balance between the exhilaration and the risks of trading, as well as how to avoid the frequent pitfalls that so many traders fall into.

The Excitement of Trading

Let us start with the obvious: trading is exciting. It's a fast-paced environment where everything can change in an instant, and the prospect of turning a little investment into a substantial return in a matter of hours, if not minutes, is quite enticing. Since there is a chance of profit or loss on every trade, every choice feels significant. The continual tension between risk and reward can provide traders with an adrenaline rush that is nearly addictive.

When I initially started trading, I was riveted to my screen, monitoring every tick and movement. The excitement was palpable—each trade represented a new chance to win big. In the beginning, I got some good wins, which boosted my enthusiasm. I began to feel that I possessed a natural ability for trading and that I was somehow unique among all those who had failed before me. But this exhilaration quickly transformed into overconfidence, and the real difficulties began.

Many traders, particularly beginners, become caught up in this emotional high. The initial gains can provide a false sense of security, making you believe that the markets are a rapid path to prosperity. When you're on a winning streak, it's easy to forget about risk management concepts because you believe the market will constantly move in your favor. However, trading is a long-term game, and markets are unpredictable. When you believe you've "figured it out," you're usually going to confront a painful reality.

The Risks of Overconfidence and Greed

One of the greatest risks in trading is the sense of invincibility that often follows a string of winning trades. Overconfidence can lead to risky moves, such as raising position size, ignoring stop losses, or entering trades outside of your strategy because you believe you can't lose. The market has a tendency to humble even the most experienced traders, and it did so with me.

I recall a particular trade that exemplifies this danger. I was riding high after a streak of great trades and decided to open a considerably larger position than I normally would. The setup seemed terrific, and I was confident that I had mastered the market. I ignored my risk management guidelines, assuming that if the trade went against me, I could handle it. Unfortunately, the market swung abruptly in the opposite way, and because I had taken on more risk than I could afford, I ended up losing not only the profits from my earlier trades but also a large chunk of my cash. It was a difficult lesson in humility and risk management, one I will never forget.

This is where the risk of greed arises. When you begin to concentrate on how much money you could make rather than focusing on executing your strategy with discipline, you are setting yourself up for failure. Greed blinds you to the hazards involved, and instead of making smart, well-thought-out trades, you begin to chase rewards. In the long run, this technique results in huge losses.

The Emotional Rollercoaster

Trading is an emotional rollercoaster. Emotions can vary wildly in a short period of time, from the high of a successful trade to the gut-wrenching sorrow of a loss. If you're not careful, these emotions can take over your decision-making process, causing you to act rashly rather than rationally. Traders frequently pursue losses, attempting to recoup losses through riskier trades. This frequently results in a cycle of compounded losses.

During my early trading days, I frequently fell into this trap. After a large loss, I would experience an overwhelming desire to return to the market, confident that I could "make it all back" with the next trade. However, trading based on emotion rather than a sound strategy almost always led to additional losses. It took me a long time to realize that the best way to respond to a lost trade is to walk away, clear your head, and then re-enter the market when you're thinking clearly and logically.

The Thin Line Between Discipline and Impulsivity

Staying disciplined is one of the most difficult aspects of trading. Discipline entails sticking to your trading strategy, according to your risk management guidelines, and not allowing emotions to influence your actions. It entails accepting losses as they occur and not attempting to "revenge trade" your way back to profitability. However, when the adrenaline is flowing, and the stakes are high, it can be extremely difficult to maintain discipline.

I've seen traders, including myself, abandon their strategies because they get caught up in the moment. A quick market movement, a piece of breaking news, or even the fear of losing out on a good opportunity can all lead to rash judgments that contradict your best judgment. When you trade on impulse rather than following a carefully constructed strategy, trading becomes perilous.

Finding Balance.

Long-term trading success requires striking a balance between excitement and caution. Trading will always have highs and lows, but the traders who thrive are those who can control their emotions and remain disciplined even when things get difficult. This does not imply that trading becomes uninteresting or that you lose interest in the markets—it simply means that you learn to channel that excitement in a way that improves rather than degrades your performance.

To accomplish this, you must focus on cultivating a mindset that values consistency over rapid rewards. Know that trading is a marathon, not a sprint. There will be good and poor days, but the traders who can keep their cool, adhere to their strategy, and avoid the temptations of overconfidence, greed, and impulsiveness will win in the long run.

Finally, the allure of trading is both its most appealing feature and its most dangerous. Understanding these pitfalls and making efforts to manage your emotions can allow you to enjoy the thrill of trading while limiting the risk. Remember that trading is more than simply generating money; it's about conquering yourself and learning to remain disciplined in the face of uncertainty. That is the actual route to success.

CHAPTER FOUR

Take Responsibility for Your Trades

Trading involves huge stakes and unknown outcomes. In this volatile climate, one of the most important lessons a trader can learn is the value of accepting complete responsibility for their actions. This chapter will look at the importance of accountability in trading, how it allows you to keep mental control, and how accepting responsibility can help you develop a more reliable trading mindset.

Accountability in Trading: No Blame, Only Ownership

When I first started trading, I was eager for immediate profits. I researched numerous strategies, tracked market patterns, and attempted to emulate the approaches of successful traders. However, I frequently found myself blaming the market for my failures. If a trade failed, it was due to unexpected news, market manipulation, or just bad luck. It took me a long to discover that this thinking was a trap that kept me trapped in a loop of disappointment.

Taking ownership is acknowledging that you are the creator of your trading strategies. Every purchase or sale order displays your judgment and strategy. If you win, it is a credit to your abilities. If you lose, it is an opportunity to learn. This shift in perspective is vital. Instead of considering setbacks as failures, consider them as stepping stones toward success.

I remember a terrible trade. Fear of missing out on potential earnings led me to take a position after conducting a quick analysis. When the trade went against me, I panicked and closed the position at a substantial loss. I instantly blamed the market for its unpredictability, unwilling to admit that my rash decision-making was the main reason for my failure.

Over time, I learned to question my decisions rather than deflect blame. I began keeping a trading notebook, in which I methodically recorded my thoughts, emotions, and the reasoning behind each trade. This practice revealed patterns in my behavior and identified places for growth. By accepting responsibility for my judgments, I improved my ability to analyze trades and make required adjustments.

How Responsibility Contributes to Mental Control

Taking responsibility for your trading decisions has a direct correlation with developing mental control. When you acknowledge that the outcomes of your trades are the product of your decisions, you obtain a sense of control. This approach is essential for remaining calm in the face of market turbulence.

In my early days, I had emotional ups and downs. A streak of good trades would boost my confidence, allowing me to make riskier judgments. Conversely, a few losses would send me into a tailspin, clouding my judgment and making me reconsider my strategy. Traders frequently experience a cycle of highs and lows, but by accepting responsibility, you can build a more stable mental state.

Understanding how your mental state affects your trading outcomes is critical. When you are responsible, you can create a framework for judging your performance that is not based on feelings. You can examine your trades objectively, learning from your failures and applauding your victories.

One day, following a string of bad trades, I became overwhelmed with frustration. Instead of reacting immediately, I took a step back. I went over my journal entries, assessed my thought process, and pondered on my decision-making habits. This self-reflection helped me regain control of my emotions. I recognized I was trading based on fear and worry rather than analysis and strategy.

Let Go of External Factors: News and Market Noise

Another important component of accepting responsibility in trading is learning to let go of external events outside your control. Market news, economic reports, and geopolitical developments can all cause disruptions in your trading strategy. While staying informed is critical, it's also important to remember that you have no control over how the market reacts to these developments.

Throughout my trading career, I discovered that I frequently exploited external factors as an explanation for bad performance. When I lost money due to unexpected news, I would tell myself that I couldn't have predicted the outcome. However, this attitude proved unproductive. Instead of focusing on what I could control—my analysis and decisions—I let outside noise determine my emotional reactions.

I gradually learned to filter out distractions. Rather than reacting rashly to news headlines, I began focusing on my trading strategy, which had been painstakingly built based on analysis. This change allowed me to stay "in the zone," making judgments based on my strategy rather than extraneous pressures.

Letting go of extraneous circumstances entails trusting your analysis and judgment. It's about having the discipline to stick to your plan despite market turbulence. As you become aware that you are capable of navigating the market's complexities without letting outside forces influence you, this discipline gives you a sense of empowerment.

Developing Self-Reliance: Trusting Your Trading Plan

The final piece of the jigsaw in accepting responsibility is developing self-reliance. Trusting your trading plan involves believing in your strategy and the actions you make based on it. This confidence stems from rigorous analysis, ongoing learning, and accepting your individual trading approach.

It was scary to create my first detailed trading plan. I was unsure whether I could stick to it. However, when I performed my trades according to plan, I gained confidence in my talents. I discovered that my strategy reflected both my expertise in the market and my psychological strengths.

Self-reliance in trading is having the conviction to stick to your plan even when the market is volatile. It is about realizing that you have the tools and expertise to succeed. This sense of self-trust allows you to make decisions that are in line with your objectives rather than succumbing to fear or doubt.

Finally, accepting responsibility for your trades is a revolutionary step in your trading experience. By accepting accountability, you gain mental control, learn to block out extraneous distractions, and develop self-reliance. These concepts will not only improve your trading success but also help you grow as a trader.

CHAPTER FIVE

Consistency, the Ultimate Mental State.

In the ever-changing world of trading, consistency is a sought-after but frequently elusive attribute. In the face of market volatility, many traders struggle with their ability to maintain a consistent approach. However, establishing consistency entails more than simply executing a trading strategy; it also entails developing a disciplined attitude that supports your trading objectives. In this chapter, we will look at the key elements of consistency, how emotional stability affects it, and practical ways to build and maintain a consistent trading mindset.

Create a Consistent Trading Process

Trading in The Zone

The sheer number of strategies and techniques available to me when I first started trading was overwhelming. I experimented with everything from day trading to long-term investing, frequently switching between approaches depending on transient trends and other people's suggestions. This lack of consistency not only hampered my performance but also left me feeling confused and frustrated.

Establishing a disciplined trading procedure is critical to developing consistency. This entails developing a routine that covers everything from analysis and execution to evaluation and adjustment. A well-defined trading process serves as a blueprint, guiding you through each stage of your trading adventure.

For example, I started creating a checklist before entering any trade. This checklist contained my entry and exit criteria, the risk-reward ratio, and the specific analysis I performed. By using this checklist, I developed a framework that ensured I made informed judgments rather than rash ones. This systematic strategy allowed me to trade with purpose and clarity, which led to better results.

Consistency and Emotional Stability

One of the major barriers to consistency is emotional volatility. Trading can cause a range of emotions, including excitement, fear, hope, and frustration. These emotions can easily obscure your judgment, resulting in rash decision-making.

During my early trading days, I personally witnessed the emotional ups and downs that come with trading. After a few winning trades, I felt invincible and began to take bigger chances. In contrast, a succession of losses caused me to doubt my talents. This emotional rollercoaster impacted my consistency; I was either overconfident or overly cautious, neither of which resulted in stable performance.

Emotional stability is essential for consistent trading. Developing emotional management strategies can greatly improve your ability to stick to your trading strategy. Techniques like mindfulness and meditation can assist you in maintaining a balanced state of mind. By using these approaches on a daily basis, I discovered that I was able to approach each trading day with a sharper perspective, allowing me to make reasonable judgments without being swayed by emotions.

The Function of Routine in Mental Strength

Routine trading is essential for developing mental strength and consistency. Establishing a daily trading routine can help you gain a sense of stability and control, allowing you to approach the market confidently.

During my journey, I learned the power of ritual. Each trading day, I set aside time for market analysis, which included reviewing economic news, technical indicators, and charts. This consistent practice enabled me to enter the market with a well-informed perspective, lowering the likelihood of making rash decisions.

In addition to pre-trade procedures, post-trade reviews are equally crucial. After each trading session, I would reflect on my trades, determining what went well and what could be better. This activity not only reinforced my learning but also helped me see trends in my behavior, allowing me to fine-tune my approach.

By implementing these routines into my trading practice, I developed a disciplined attitude that promoted consistency. Each day felt purposeful, and I could approach the market with confidence rather than turmoil.

How to Develop a Consistent Trading Mindset

Developing a consistent trading mindset necessitates ongoing work and self-awareness. *Here are some practical strategies for cultivating a mentality that values consistency:*

- ➢ ***Set Specific Goals:*** Determine both short-term and long-term trading objectives. Having defined objectives helps to guide your decisions and keep you focused on the overall strategy.

- ➢ *Create a Trading Journal:* Keeping a notebook where you record your trades, emotions, and ideas might yield insightful feedback. Reflecting on your experiences helps you recognize patterns, successes, and opportunities for development.

- ➢ *Adopt a Growth Mindset:* Look at every trade as a learning opportunity, regardless of the outcome. Adopting a growth mindset cultivates resilience and adaptability, both of which are required for consistent performance.

- ➢ *Limit Distractions:* In today's information-rich world, it's easy to feel overwhelmed. Limit your sources of information to those that are consistent with your trading philosophy, and avoid excessive noise that can impair your judgment.

- ➤ **_Practice Patience:_** Consistency is not about rushing into trades; it is about waiting for the appropriate chances that fit your strategy. Trust the process and allow yourself time to improve your talents.

- ➤ **_Review and Modify Your Plan Often:_** Your trading strategy should change along with the market. Regularly evaluate your performance and make modifications as needed to stay on track with your objectives.

As I applied these strategies to my trading practice, I noticed a considerable improvement in my performance. I shifted from chaotic decision-making to a more consistent approach. This newfound stability enabled me to better weather the market's inevitable ups and downs.

Finally, constancy is the ideal mental state that every trader should strive for. You can improve your trading performance by constructing a disciplined trading process, practicing emotional stability, establishing a habit, and adopting a consistent attitude. Remember that trading is more than just making money; it's also about developing a long-term strategy that promotes growth and success. Stay devoted to the process, and you will discover that consistency becomes a valuable asset in your trading career.

CHAPTER SIX

The Dynamics of Perception in Trading

In trading, perception is essential. As a trader, your perception of the market influences your decisions more than any technical or fundamental analysis. At times, perception can blind us to reality, making it difficult to differentiate between opportunity and risk. In this chapter, we'll look at how perception influences decision-making, identify typical biases that affect traders, and discover how to match our mentality with market realities to increase trading performance.

How Perception Drives Decision-Making.

When I first started trading, I was preoccupied with finding the perfect trading strategy. I'd spend hours analyzing charts, looking for patterns that guaranteed riches. Despite my best efforts, I would frequently enter trades too late or exit them too early. It wasn't until I understood my market perception was wrong that I made significant progress.

Perception is the lens through which we see the market, and it is shaped by our emotions, beliefs, and previous experiences. For instance, if you've experienced a string of losses, fear may cloud your perception and cause you to perceive risk when there is none. Conversely, after a string of victories, overconfidence may cause you to perceive the market as less risky than it is, leading you to take needless risks.

The key to good trading is to understand how your perception influences your decisions. Rather than depending simply on gut impulses or emotions, you must base your perception on facts and objective analysis. This entails regularly assessing the market based on facts rather than feelings.

Detecting Biases and False Perceptions in Trading

Every trader has biases—mental shortcuts that can muddle judgment and distort decision-making. Some of these biases arise from our natural human dispositions, while others emerge as a result of our market experiences. Recognizing these biases is the first step toward reducing their effects.

One of the most common biases I experienced early in my trading career was confirmation bias. I would frequently enter trades based on a specific thesis and then search out evidence that supported my belief while ignoring data that disputed it. This bias not only forced me to hold losing trades for longer than necessary, but it also kept me from seeing new chances.

Another key prejudice is recency bias, in which we place more emphasis on recent events or trades than on the big picture. After having a winning streak, I became complacent, expecting that my success would last indefinitely. I failed to examine broader market patterns, resulting in losses when market conditions moved.

False perceptions can also result from seeing patterns that do not exist, which is known as pattern recognition bias. Our minds are predisposed to look for patterns in even the most random data, which can lead to poor trading judgments. For example, I would sometimes convince myself that a price movement mirrored a previous trend and execute trades based on this false perception, only to discover that the market was moving in the opposite direction.

Being conscious of these biases allows you to challenge your perception of the market and make more informed judgments. You can avoid the traps of misleading perceptions by challenging your beliefs and staying grounded in objective analysis.

Perception vs. Reality: What the Market Really Says.

Particularly in trading, there can be significant differences between perception and reality. Markets are intricate and subject to numerous influences, most of which are uncontrollable for traders. It is easy to misread short-term changes as signs of long-term trends, resulting in poor trades.

In one of my previous trades, I made the error of misinterpreting a brief price drop as a long-term decrease. The news seemed grim at the time, and my perception was that the market was headed for a prolonged decline. Instead of considering the big picture, such as economic fundamentals and the general trend, I concentrated on the short term and quickly sold off my position. A few days later, the market returned, and I realized my perception had been completely incorrect.

The reality of the market frequently differs from what we perceive at the moment. Understanding this relationship is critical to successful trading. Rather than reacting to short-term swings, consider the larger context, which includes trends, market mood, and economic considerations. By aligning your perception with reality, you can avoid making hasty decisions based on insufficient facts.

Train Your Mind to See Opportunities Clearly

One of the most crucial talents a trader can develop is the ability to identify opportunities clearly, free of biases and emotions. This necessitates continued mental training and discipline.

Over the years, I've created a number of techniques to help me improve my market perception. One of the most effective strategies has been the discipline of detachment. By emotionally separating from the outcome of a trade, I am able to examine prospects more clearly. When I'm not concerned about whether I'll win or lose, I can perceive the market for what it is: a dynamic system with risks and benefits.

Another useful method is to look for alternate viewpoints. Early in my trading career, I mainly followed analysts and traders who shared my views. However, as I began to diversify my sources of knowledge, I discovered that examining diverse perspectives allowed me to identify opportunities that I had previously missed. For example, during a market slump, while I saw the situation as completely terrible, another trader saw it as an excellent opportunity for short bets. Their perspective opened up new options for me.

Meditation and mindfulness activities have also been quite beneficial in training my mind to remain focused and calm. By practicing mindfulness, I am able to examine my thoughts and feelings without allowing them to influence my actions. This has helped me maintain my composure amid volatile market situations and prevent impulsive trades motivated by fear or excitement.

In conclusion, perception is an imperceptible yet significant force that influences your trading decisions. Knowing this will help you make better informed judgments on how your perceptions influence your behavior, addressing biases, and training your mind to see the market clearly. The more closely your perception aligns with reality, the more profitable and consistent your trading will be. You can develop the mental clarity required to navigate markets with confidence and precision via consistent practice and self-awareness.

CHAPTER SEVEN

Understanding the Market's Perspective.

One of the most important lessons I've learned from trading is the value of knowing the market's perspective. As traders, we frequently become preoccupied with our own analysis, concentrating on charts, indicators, and economic information. While these tools are essential, they only provide a portion of the picture. To fully excel, we must grasp how the market works from a collective psychological perspective—how fear, greed, and crowd behavior affect price movements.

The marketplace is not a rational entity. It reflects people's emotions, expectations, and reactions. As much as we would like to believe that technical analysis and economic fundamentals determine pricing, market sentiment frequently dictates short-term changes. In this chapter, we'll look at the market's collective psychology, how it responds to emotions, and how to align your attitude with its movements.

Understanding the Market Through the Lens of Collective Psychology

One of the most eye-opening events of my trading career came in the aftermath of a significant geopolitical incident. The market was in disarray—prices were wildly moving, and news channels were blasting us with conflicting information. I had my analysis prepared, but nothing seemed to make sense. The price was not moving according to logic or fundamentals;

rather, it was reacting to the collective psychology of fear.

This incident taught me an important lesson: the market is driven by the emotions of its participants. When traders feel fear, they sell assets in a frenzy, typically regardless of their inherent value. When greed takes over, individuals buy into rallies, driving prices higher and higher, often much above what any sensible analysis would predict. Understanding this behavior allows you to better predict market moves and, more crucially, avoid becoming emotionally involved yourself.

One way to begin seeing the market from this perspective is to focus on the concept of market sentiment. Sentiment indicates traders' overall mood, indicating whether they are optimistic or pessimistic about the market's trajectory. It can be measured using instruments such as sentiment indexes, news reports, and even social media trends. While technical and fundamental analysis can tell you where the market "should" move, knowing your mood can help you predict where it will go in the short term.

How Markets Respond to Human Emotions

In many respects, the market reflects our collective feelings. Traders, whether amateurs or seasoned professionals, all contribute to market behavior by their behaviors, which are driven by emotional triggers such as fear, greed, and uncertainty.

Take, for example, the 2008 financial crisis. The fall of Lehman Brothers caused widespread panic in the markets, resulting in a major sell-off. While economic fundamentals played a role in the collapse, fear was the primary driver of the market's decline. Fearing greater losses, investors rushed to sell, driving prices down and lower in a self-reinforcing spiral.

On the other hand, enthusiasm and greed are frequently what drive market rallies. When consumers see others making money, they want in on the activity, which drives prices up as they buy into the trend. This is usually when bubbles form. One particular story comes to mind: I traded in the cryptocurrency market during the 2017 Bitcoin surge. Prices rose when more retail traders entered the market, motivated by fear of missing out (FOMO). Even though there were strong signals that the market was overheated, many traders, including myself, were too excited to notice the inevitable correction.

Markets are driven by human emotions rather than pure rationality, and understanding this provides you with a significant advantage. Rather than attempting to outwit the market, it is frequently more successful in aligning with its emotional beat.

Understanding Market Sentiment and Crowd Behavior.

Crowd behavior is one of the most interesting parts of market psychology. Markets frequently move in herds, with big groups of traders following similar patterns based on shared emotions. This explains why we witness bubbles and busts that defy fundamentals.

Herding behavior is an excellent example of this phenomenon. In the stock market, for example, when a well-known analyst or financial figure makes a big prediction, thousands of traders may follow suit, driving the market in a specific direction. Even if the advice is incorrect, the sheer volume of trades can result in a self-fulfilling prophecy.

Understanding this might help you recognize instances of irrational enthusiasm or panic. You can take a step back when you notice that strong emotions are driving the market, such as the rush to buy into a stock that is rapidly rising or a panic-driven sell-off during a downturn. Instead of joining the crowd, approach the matter rationally. These emotional market extremes frequently present opportunities—either to sell at the pinnacle of a rally or to buy when everyone else is too terrified.

Another personal experience that taught me this lesson occurred during the 2020 pandemic market crisis. At the height of the panic, I witnessed major indices plummet in a matter of days. Fear had sent the market into freefall. However, after taking a step back and evaluating the issue objectively, I recognized there was an opportunity. Rather than panic selling, I methodically entered positions that I considered were undervalued, and those trades were successful as the market recovered.

Adapting Your Mindset to Market Trends

To become a consistently winning trader, you must be emotionally and strategically aligned with market movements. This does not imply getting caught up in the crowd's emotions but rather recognizing when emotions are at play and leveraging them to your advantage.

One strategy that has proven effective for me is emotional detachment. You can examine trends objectively and without letting popular opinion influence you by taking a step back from the market's emotional highs and lows. Meditation and mindfulness have been really helpful for me in achieving emotional distance. They help me to observe market trends without being engrossed in the day-to-day volatility.

Another crucial part of market alignment is taking a long-term perspective. It's easy to get caught up in short-term market noise, but effective traders understand the broader picture. When you grasp the fundamental market trend, you're less inclined to make rash decisions based on fleeting emotional swings.

For example, during the 2021 stock market bull run, I concentrated on timing my trades with the overall market rise. Instead of getting caught up in day-to-day volatility, I relied on my analysis of the overall trend and held my positions even when the market briefly fell. This method was significantly more profitable than reacting to slight fluctuations.

Knowing the market's perspective is critical for long-term trading success. Recognizing the impact of collective psychology, learning to sense market sentiment, and avoiding emotional reactions can give you a substantial advantage. Aligning your attitude with the market enables you to remain grounded and make sensible, informed judgments even when emotions are high. The more you grasp the market's emotional dynamics, the more prepared you will be to weather its ups and downs.

Trading in The Zone

CHAPTER EIGHT

The Trader's Perspective: Examining Chances

Many people enter trading with the idea of being able to accurately predict the market. They believe that by conducting extensive technical analysis and researching price fluctuations, they would be able to develop a flawless system that will predict where the market will go. However, trading is about probability, not certainty. Successful traders do not strive for perfection; instead, they focus on risk management and making judgments based on the likelihood of outcomes.

Learning to think in probabilities is essential for gaining a competitive advantage in the market. This mindset adjustment distinguishes amateur traders from pros. It is not about predicting with 100% accuracy but rather about entering trades when the odds are in your favor and limiting your risk when they are not.

Trading in the Zone: Probability-Based Thinking

When I initially started trading, I was preoccupied with being correct. I'd spend many hours improving my technical analysis, looking for the holy grail of indications that would predict where the market would go. Despite my best efforts, I was left feeling frustrated. I would become emotional when trades went against me as if I had done something wrong. Things only started to change after I learned to embrace uncertainty and think in probabilities.

You will never be 100% correct in trading. Losses are unavoidable. But that's fine because the goal isn't perfection. The idea is to earn more on winning trades than you do on losing trades. Thinking in probabilities allows you to recognize that losses are inevitable rather than attempting to prevent them entirely.

Imagine you are flipping a coin. You won't consistently receive a heads-tails pattern when you flip the coin, even if it is fair and lands head 50% of the time and tails 50% of the time. Sometimes, you get three heads, sometimes two tails. However, if you continue to flip the coin, the outcomes will eventually even out to 50-50. Trading works similarly. Individual trades may not always go your way, but if you adhere to a strategy with a positive expectation, you'll come out ahead over time.

Overcoming the Certainty Trap and Embracing Risk

One of the most common mistakes beginning traders make is falling into the certainty trap. They believe that with enough information, they can completely remove risk. However, trading is inherently risky. Every trade you make involves risk, and no amount of analysis can change that.

Early in my trading career, I had a disastrous encounter. I was confident that the market would break out in a specific direction. I had completed all of my homework, including poring over charts, checking economic news, and consulting any indication I could think of. I went all-in on the trade, thinking I had eliminated all ambiguity. But then, as is often the case, the market reversed itself. I watched in horror as my account balance dropped, all because I was certain I was correct.

That event taught me a difficult but important lesson: there are no guarantees in trading. The market does not care how much you have researched or how certain you are in your analysis. What matters is that you understand that every trade involves risk, and it is your responsibility to manage that risk rather than eradicate it.

To embrace risk means accepting that you have no control over the market; you only have power over how you react to it. This entails becoming comfortable with the idea of incurring losses. It entails not overleveraging yourself or risking too much on a single trade. You can stay in the game long enough to let your edge play out by thinking in probabilities and accepting risk.

How to Create a Probability-Based Trading Strategy

Building a probability-based trading strategy entails focusing on settings where the probabilities are in your favor. It does not imply that you must win every trade; rather, over time, your winners should outnumber your losers. One method to accomplish this is to ensure your trades have a favorable risk-to-reward ratio.

The risk-to-reward ratio is a simple idea. If you risk $100 on a trade, you should expect to make at least $200 in return. This means that even if you only win half of your trades, you'll still be profitable because your wins are twice as large as your losers.

Assume you enter a trade and set a stop loss of 50 pips (your risk). Your aim is 100 pips (reward). This yields a 2:1 risk-to-reward ratio. Even if you lose as many trades as you win, you'll still come out ahead because your winners will offset your losses.

In addition to a favorable risk-to-reward ratio, back-testing your strategy is critical. Back-testing entails reviewing historical data to determine how your strategy would have fared in the past. While past performance does not always predict future results, back-testing can give you confidence that your strategy will perform well over time.

Mental Exercises to Strengthen Probability Thinking

Transitioning to a probability mindset is easier said than done. Taking losses is one of the most difficult emotional parts of trading for many traders. It's crucial to train your brain to think in probabilities because of this.

One of the most useful mental exercises I've discovered is to treat each trade as a single event in a long series of trades. Instead of concentrating on the outcome of a single trade, consider your performance over the next 100 trades. This allows you to disconnect emotionally from specific outcomes while remaining focused on the big picture.

Another beneficial exercise is to practice visualizing. Before entering a trade, consider both the best and worst-case possibilities. Imagine yourself managing both outcomes with calmness and composure. This prepares your mind for the emotional reactions that are common when trading, as well as reinforces the idea that any single trade is only a minor portion of the entire process.

CHAPTER NINE

Managing Your Beliefs for Trading Success

Our beliefs impact how we perceive the world, make decisions, and respond to diverse situations. In trading, your beliefs determine not only your strategy but also how you react to success and defeat. These deep-seated ideas, whether you're conscious of them or not, govern your trading actions, so identifying and understanding them is crucial.

Many people believe that technical or fundamental analysis is the sole determinant of trading success. While understanding of market mechanics is vital, what truly distinguishes successful traders is the psychological base upon which they operate. In other words, your views can determine the success or failure of your trading profession.

Identifying and Analyzing Core Beliefs for Trading

Every trader enters the market with a set of core beliefs, either conscious or subconscious, that influence how they approach their trades. Some people believe that the market is intrinsically fair, while others believe that it is working against them. Some believe that generating money in trading is all about luck, while others believe it is entirely skill-based. Whatever your beliefs are, they influence every decision you make when trading.

To determine your underlying beliefs, consider your initial thoughts and feelings following both a winning and losing trade. Do you feel lucky when you win? Do you blame external causes, such as market manipulation or negative news, for your losses? These thought patterns indicate the beliefs that motivate your actions.

A few years into my trading career, I discovered a hidden belief that was hurting my success. After a string of losses, I would be extremely wary of entering another trade, even if my strategy indicated a fantastic opportunity. The fear of losing was linked to a strong conviction that I was not "cut out" to be a good trader. Only after identifying and fighting this notion was I able to persevere and reclaim my confidence.

By becoming aware of the beliefs that drive your decision-making, you will be able to determine which ones are working for you and which are holding you back.

How Your Beliefs Influence Your Trading Behavior.

Your beliefs shape how you interpret market data and trading signals. If you believe the market is uncertain and chaotic, you may hesitate to enter trades or switch from one strategy to another in search of something more solid. On the other hand, if you believe that the market offers opportunities to those who are disciplined and patient, you are more likely to stick to your strategy through thick and thin.

Let's imagine you feel that if you find the right signal, you can win every trade. This belief may cause you to spend many hours optimizing your system, attempting to remove all losses. However, no strategy can guarantee a 100 percent win rate. The pursuit of perfection may drive you to pass up profitable prospects merely because you are waiting for certainty.

Another example is the expectation of instant pleasure. Many traders enter the market expecting to get wealthy immediately. If you believe this, you're more likely to take unnecessary risks or trade recklessly in search of rapid returns. The truth, however, is that trading success needs time, patience, and discipline. If you do not change this belief, it is only a matter of time before you suffer major losses.

When I initially started trading, I assumed that if I worked hard enough, I could forecast every market action. This caused me to overanalyze every chart, looking for the "perfect" arrangement. However, I soon learned that this belief was inaccurate and damaging to my trading performance. My trading outcomes increased considerably after I accepted that I didn't need to predict the market with perfect accuracy but rather manage risk and be consistent.

How to Change Limiting Beliefs to Gain a Psychological Advantage.

Once you've discovered the beliefs that are holding you back, the next step is to transform those limiting beliefs into ones that will help you succeed. This isn't always easy because many of our main beliefs are strongly formed, typically as a result of childhood or early adult events. However, with deliberate effort and practice, you may alter the way you think and, as a result, the way you trade.

Affirmations and visualization are excellent strategies for altering limiting beliefs. For example, if you believe you are incapable of trading successfully, start each day with the affirmation, "I am a skilled and disciplined trader. I believe in my strategy and remain calm under pressure." Repeating this statement over time can assist in reorganizing your brain, replacing negative, limiting thoughts with more empowered ones.

Another technique is to use evidence to challenge your beliefs. If you assume that you must win every trade to be successful, consider your previous trading performance. Do you have evidence that your total success is not dependent on a 100% victory rate? This type of critical examination assists in dismantling limiting ideas and replacing them with more constructive ones.

I originally thought that suffering a loss meant I had failed as a trader. This belief would send me into an emotional spiral after each losing trade, which frequently led to revenge trading—a dangerous habit in which you place hasty trades to "get back" what you lost. After several months of this conduct, I understood my belief was fundamentally incorrect. I began to see the wider picture—how each trade was only one among hundreds of trades I'd make during the year.

Shifting my mindset from "losses are failures" to "losses are part of the process" enabled me to remain calm and committed to my strategy even after a losing streak.

Developing Positive Trading Beliefs for Long-Term Success

The third phase is to reinforce positive thoughts that will benefit you in the long run. These are ideas that are consistent with good trading behaviors, such as patience, discipline, and resilience. Strengthening these ideas will allow you to keep a psychological advantage in the markets even when conditions become difficult.

One of the most effective positive beliefs you can nurture is that trading success is based on consistency rather than perfection. This belief helps you stick to your trading strategy even when individual trades don't go your way. It prevents you from overreacting to short-term results and encourages you to concentrate on the process rather than the end.

Another positive concept to cultivate is the notion that you are in control of your actions, not the market. You cannot control how the market moves, but you can influence how you react to those movements. This belief promotes personal accountability and encourages you to accept responsibility for your trades rather than blaming external forces.

I remember a time when I had a string of successful trades. My confidence grew, and I began to believe that I could do no wrong. This inflated sense of assurance caused me to take on more risk than I should have, and as expected, the market humbled me with a substantial loss. That event taught me the value of humility and the idea that the market is always bigger than any individual trader. Strengthening this belief has kept me grounded and focused on risk management, regardless of how many victories I accumulate.

Finally, your beliefs will determine your trading success. By identifying limiting ideas, replacing them with more empowering ones, and reinforcing positive beliefs, you can create the mentality required for long-term trading success.

CHAPTER TEN

The Nature of Belief in Trading

In the world of trading, the concept of "belief" may appear abstract at first. Many traders rely solely on technical indicators, market movements, and fundamental analysis. However, your beliefs, whether conscious or subconscious, influence every decision you make. Whether you realize it or not, your mindset is influenced by these beliefs, which affect your behaviors, reactions, and, eventually, your trading results.

The nature of beliefs in trading is important since they are the lenses through which we observe the market. They influence our perceptions and guide our decisions. If you're on a losing streak or keep making the same mistakes, it's time to examine the beliefs that motivate your actions. This chapter investigates how beliefs are created, how they influence trading, and how to change them for improved performance.

Formation of Belief in the Mind

Experiences, repetition, and reinforcement all contribute to the formation of beliefs over time. These experiences may be from childhood, previous employment, or early trading encounters. In trading, beliefs are frequently formed based on early victories or losses. A trader who has a substantial win early in their career may develop the belief that the market is "easy" and underestimate the hazards. On the other hand, a trader who suffers a series of losses may tend to believe that trading success is out of reach, or worse, that the market is "rigged" against them.

My own trading career was largely affected by the belief that hard work and intelligence alone could ensure success. Coming from an academic background where effort was directly tied to results, I believed that if I spent enough time studying charts and strategies, I could understand the market. However, the market does not work that way. After a spate of losses, I recognized that my belief in the direct effort-result correlation was incorrect. In trading, success is typically determined by emotional control rather than technical ability.

Beliefs are also reinforced by repetition. When you consistently observe great outcomes from a particular action, you begin to assume it is the "right" way. This is why many traders become overconfident after a few winning trades. They feel they have "figured out" the market, only to be humbled when market conditions change.

How Subconscious Beliefs Impact Trading Decisions

One of the most difficult things of trading is that many of our beliefs are subconscious. These subconscious beliefs frequently appear in subtle ways, influencing our decisions without our awareness. For example, if you subconsciously believe that money is scarce, you may abandon profitable trades too early, fearing that the market would turn against you. Conversely, if you believe that taking high risks is the only way to win big, you may disregard good risk management methods and over-leverage your trades.

For a long time, I functioned under the subconscious belief that losses were a reflection of my trade talents. This belief made me extra cautious and unwilling to execute high-probability trades. After a series of wasted opportunities, I began to wonder why I was so frightened. It wasn't until I looked into my subconscious beliefs that I understood I was associating a lost trade with personal failure. When I became aware of this belief, I sought to reframe it and decouple my self-worth from certain trade outcomes.

Subconscious beliefs are difficult to recognize, but they frequently emerge when you pay attention to emotional reactions when trading. For example, if you experience a strong emotional response—whether fear, anxiety, or excitement—when entering or departing a trade, it could indicate that a subconscious belief is impacting your decision.

Beliefs and the Development of Confidence

Confidence in trading has a double edge. Too little confidence might paralyze you, causing you to pass up possibilities, but too much confidence can lead to rash decisions. The aim is to cultivate balanced confidence, and beliefs play an important part in accomplishing this goal.

When your beliefs are in line with reality, you can be confident in your trade talents. This kind of confidence is not based on the outcome of a particular trade, but rather on the consistency of your process. For example, knowing that the market is unpredictable but that you can manage your risk permits you to trade confidently, especially during tumultuous times. You don't rely on certainty for success; rather, you believe in your ability to handle whatever the market throws at you.

I remember a moment when I lacked the courage to trust my trading strategy. After a few losses, I began questioning every trade, even when the setup seemed obvious. My belief was that if a trade failed, it indicated a fault in my strategy. This belief harmed my confidence and prompted me to hesitate, resulting in the loss of numerous profitable trades. My confidence did not return until I changed my belief from "I must be right on every trade" to "My job is to follow my plan and manage risk." With this new belief, I was able to approach each trade calmly and focused, knowing that losses were unavoidable.

Changing Negative Beliefs for Better Performance

The most essential conclusion from the nature of beliefs in trading is that they may be altered. Negative beliefs, if uncontrolled, will continue to undermine your performance. However, you can replace them with empowering, positive beliefs that will help you succeed if you put in the necessary information and work.

The first step toward changing a bad belief is to acknowledge it. This necessitates self-awareness and honesty. Once you've found the belief that's holding you back, consider if it's beneficial to you. For example, if you feel that making money in trading is simply a matter of luck, consider whether this belief is benefiting or harming your success. Most likely, it is causing you to be inconsistent or overly reliant on luck rather than ability.

The following step is to reframe the negative belief. Instead of believing that trading success is based on luck, you might embrace the following belief: "Trading success is based on consistency, discipline, and risk management." This belief allows you to concentrate on what you can manage rather than feeling at the mercy of the market.

I used to hold the belief that before making a trade, I needed to comprehend all of the market factors. This belief led to analysis paralysis, in which I would spend hours overanalyzing data and overlook the best entry points. Over time, I reframed this belief as "I don't need to know everything, I just need to follow my plan and manage risk." This shift in belief enabled me to enter trades with greater confidence and less reluctance.

Finally, reinforce your new belief with repetition and practice. The more you act in line with your new belief, the stronger it will become. Over time, your subconscious will accept this belief as the new normal, and it will begin to influence your behavior in beneficial ways.

Beliefs are the basis of your trading attitude, and knowing their nature is critical to your success. Understanding your fundamental beliefs, evaluating how they affect your trading, and working to change your negative beliefs into positive ones can help you become the best trader you can be. Remember that while you cannot control the market, you can control your beliefs, attitudes, and actions. Your chances of long-term trading success increase with how closely your goals and beliefs align.

Trading in The Zone

CHAPTER ELEVEN

The Effect of Beliefs on Trading Results

Beliefs impact your reality, behaviors, and outcomes, whether you are conscious of them or not. In trading, this principle is even more important because every decision is dependent on your own framework of beliefs. Some beliefs benefit you, while others can hold you back. Being able to reinterpret your limiting beliefs and comprehend how they affect your trading results is essential to becoming a consistently profitable trader.

How Beliefs Can Improve or Disrupt Trading Results

Beliefs are the internal laws by which we live and function. In trading, your beliefs about the market, money, and even yourself influence your performance. Positive beliefs can improve your ability to maintain discipline, manage risk, and execute trades with precision. Conversely, negative or restricting beliefs can cause self-sabotage, such as emotional trading, poor risk management, or rash actions.

Early in my trading career, I had a firmly established belief that I had to be correct on every trade. This belief stemmed from a fear of failure that I gained from previous experiences in which I associated mistakes with personal inferiority. Because of this belief, I was extremely cautious, unwilling to execute trades that weren't a "sure thing." This thinking caused me to miss numerous opportunities, and when I did enter a trade, I would withdraw too soon in order to avoid the possibility of being incorrect.

As a result, my trading performance was average, at best. Despite having a good strategy, my fear-based belief system was preventing me from seizing the chances in front of me. It wasn't until I questioned and reframed this belief—understanding that losses are a normal part of the trading process—that I noticed an improvement in my performance. Shifting my thinking to focus on probability rather than being correct provided me with the mental flexibility to execute my trades confidently.

On the other side, traders who have empowering beliefs about themselves and the market might employ those beliefs to improve their trading results. For example, a trader who feels that discipline and consistency are essential for trading success will concentrate on learning their profession, developing their strategies, and sticking to a trading strategy. This belief promotes long-term performance by encouraging traders to see trading as a process rather than a collection of individual events.

Examining Real-Life Case Studies of Trader Beliefs

Many successful traders have recounted their experiences with how beliefs affected their trading careers, and there are common themes in their stories. Let's look at two examples: one of self-sabotage caused by limiting beliefs and another of breakthrough success motivated by empowering beliefs.

In the first situation, I knew a trader who had a deep understanding of technical analysis. He could read charts, recognize trends, and forecast market movements with remarkable accuracy. Despite this knowledge, he failed to retain profitability. When I looked deeper into his psyche, I realized that his core belief was that he was never "good enough" to achieve. This belief had nothing to do with trading and arose from previous life situations in which he felt inadequate in other areas. He brought this belief into his trading, and it manifested itself in the way he questioned his strategies, overanalyzed his trades, and hesitated to pull the trigger.

Even when he was in a winning trade, he couldn't completely enjoy it since he was continually concerned about when it would turn against him. This caused him to abandon trades prematurely, missing out on higher gains. His belief in his own inferiority hampered his ability to perform at his full potential.

On the other hand, I've seen traders who were able to rethink their beliefs and improve their trading careers. One of the traders I taught first believed that trading was purely luck and that the market was unpredictable. This belief caused him to be unpredictable in his trades, frequently switching from one strategy to another in the hopes of "getting lucky." After we worked on changing his belief to "The market is unpredictable, but I can control my actions and manage risk," his approach drastically altered. He began focusing on the process rather than the outcome, sticking to his trading strategy and controlling his risk. This new belief enabled him to remain cool throughout market turbulence, and his outcomes increased dramatically over time.

Reframing Self-Limiting Beliefs as Empowering

One of the most effective tools you can use as a trader is the ability to redefine your beliefs. If you discover that some beliefs are holding you back, there is good news: you can modify them. Reframing a belief simply means looking at it from a different angle and figuring out how to transform it into something positive and actionable.

For example, suppose you think that "the market is too unpredictable to be consistently profitable." This belief can induce reluctance and a lack of confidence in your strategy. Instead, rephrase this belief as follows: "The market may be unpredictable, but with a solid strategy and proper risk management, I can still achieve consistent profits over time." This adjustment in mentality encourages you to focus on the things over which you have control rather than being immobilized by market uncertainty.

In my personal experience, reframing beliefs was a game changer. I used to think, "Losses mean I'm not a good trader." This belief created a fear of losing, causing me to pause on trades or quit too soon. By reframing this belief as "Losses are part of the process, and my success depends on how I manage them," I was able to disconnect emotionally from individual trades and concentrate on long-term consistency. This shift enabled me to take measured risks without fear, which enhanced my trading results.

Practical Ways to Rewire Beliefs for Success

Rewiring your beliefs requires time and conscious work, but the results are well worth it. *Here are some practical ways to reframe and reinforce good beliefs in your trading:*

- ➤ **Self-Reflection:** Spend time reflecting on your trading habits and discovering patterns. What beliefs drive your actions? Are they helping or hindering your performance?

Once you've recognized your limiting beliefs, write them down.

- ➤ ***Reframing:*** Find a method to transform each limiting belief into something positive. For example, if you believe, "I'll never be able to master trading," reframe it as "I can always improve by learning and practicing."

- ➤ ***Affirmations:*** Use everyday affirmations to strengthen your new beliefs. Write down positive sentences that are consistent with your new beliefs, and read them to yourself every day. This helps to reinforce them in your subconscious mind.

- ➤ ***Visualization:*** Imagine yourself trading successfully with your new beliefs in place. Consider how a powerful perspective would influence your actions, feelings, and decisions. Visualization can be an effective strategy for instilling new beliefs in your mind.

> ➢ *Action:* Finally, take action that is consistent with your new beliefs. If you believe, "I can manage risk and be profitable over time," then engage in trades that demonstrate good risk management. The more you act in accordance with your new beliefs, the stronger they will become.

Your beliefs are the invisible power that influences your trading decisions and results. The beliefs you have determine whether they help or hinder your endeavors. You may greatly improve your trading performance by becoming aware of these beliefs, reframing any that are restrictive, and reinforcing good, empowering beliefs. Trading is more than simply charts and strategies; it's about mastering the mental game. When you link your beliefs with your objectives, you lay the groundwork for long-term market success.

CHAPTER TWELVE

Think Like a Trader in the Zone.

Trading is more than just gaining money; it is also about developing your thinking. When you think like a trader who is "in the zone," you operate with clarity, discipline, and focus that transcends market noise. This frame of mind enables you to separate from emotions, focus on the process, and consistently make trading decisions that are consistent with your strategy. However, obtaining this mental state is not easy; it necessitates ongoing work on your psychological structure. In this chapter, we'll look at how to develop and maintain a "zone" mentality in order to achieve peak market performance.

Developing a "Zone" Mindset for Peak Performance.

What is it like to be "in the zone" as a trader? It's the mental condition in which everything runs well. You are not overthinking, second-guessing, or responding emotionally to every market fluctuation. Instead, you execute your strategy calmly, with purpose and attention. This frame of mind comes from a thorough grasp of both the market and yourself as a trader.

I can recall multiple occasions when I entered this mood, and my trades appeared to flow freely. The market was tumultuous, but I remained cool and focused on implementing my strategy. I wasn't thinking about how much I stood to gain or lose; I was simply following my process. And because I was distanced from the outcome, I made better choices. During this time, I experienced one of my most profitable streaks. I wasn't chasing profits or attempting to push trades; I was simply in sync with the market and my strategy. That is the essence of thinking like a trader in the zone.

How to Maintain Emotional Detachment from the Market

One of the most difficult aspects of trading is maintaining emotional distance from the markets. When emotions like fear, greed, and frustration interfere, your judgment becomes muddled. Traders who let their emotions guide their judgments are more likely to make rash decisions, such as departing too soon out of fear or over-leveraging due to greed.

Maintaining emotional separation requires a long-term, process-oriented perspective. Focus on the overall trading process rather than individual trade outcomes. This shift in perspective enables you to approach each trade with a clear mind, knowing that a single loss or profit is only a portion of the broader picture.

One of the ways I learned to disconnect emotionally from the market was to realize that losses are unavoidable. Early in my trading career, I dreaded losses, viewing them as personal failings. However, I learned over time that losses are a part of the game and do not define my success as a trader. This attitude enabled me to remain cool, even during losing streaks, and to concentrate on what I could control—my risk management, strategy, and discipline.

Setting explicit guidelines for your trades is another effective technique to disengage from emotions. Having a clear entry and exit strategy, combined with strong risk management, eliminates the emotional decision-making process. You know exactly when you'll enter and exit a trade, regardless of how the market swings, so your emotions stay in check.

Developing a Long-Term, Process-Oriented Mindset.

Thinking like a trader in the zone entails establishing a long-term perspective. Too many traders become fixated on short-term results, allowing a single trade to decide their confidence or decision-making process. When you focus entirely on short-term results, it's easy to become emotionally reactive—overly enthusiastic about victories or disappointed by losses.

A process-oriented attitude focuses on long-term success rather than short-term outcomes. You begin to see each trade as a modest step on a much broader journey. This allows you to be more consistent in your execution knowing that your success as a trader will be assessed over time rather than by a single trade.

Personally, I discovered that when I stopped concentrating on daily gains and instead focused on improving my trading method, my performance improved considerably. I no longer felt compelled to force trades simply to "make up" for a bad day. Instead, I executed my strategy with discipline, knowing that if I stayed to the procedure, the profits would come.

Building this mindset needs patience and a willingness to realize that not every trade will be profitable. You should also be okay with delayed gratification. In trading, the actual rewards are generally derived from compounding tiny, consistent gains over time rather than hitting the jackpot on a single trade.

Continuous Growth: Maintaining a Sharp and Adaptable Mindset.

The market is constantly evolving, and so should you. To stay in the zone as a trader, you must continually grow, learn, and adapt. Markets change, strategies lose their edge, and new possibilities emerge. If you grow complacent or dogmatic in your thinking, you will risk slipping behind.

Staying sharp as a trader necessitates a dedication to continuing education and self-analysis. Regularly evaluate your trades, not only to discover where you went wrong but also to understand what works and why. This process of self-evaluation allows you to fine-tune your strategies and make required changes.

There was a time when I was consistently losing money in my trading. I couldn't figure out what was happening because I was using the same strategies that had been effective for months. After examining my trades and monitoring the market, I understood that market conditions had changed and my strategy was no longer viable in that context. This event showed me the value of staying adaptable. I needed to change my approach to reflect the new market realities, and once I did, I was able to get back on track.

In addition to evaluating your trades, make it a practice to keep up with market trends, new strategies, and the psychological aspects of trading. Read books, take classes, and interact with other traders to extend your perspective. The more you learn, the sharper your intellect will grow, helping you to maintain your market edge.

Another critical component of continual improvement is maintaining your mindset outside of trading. Physical health, mental well-being and emotional balance all influence how well you perform as a trader. Regular exercise, mindfulness techniques, and a healthy lifestyle all contribute to your ability to stay focused and in the zone. Trading needs a high level of mental stamina, and taking care of your general health is critical to maintaining that focus over time.

Thinking like a trader in the zone is about more than just completing trades; it's about establishing a mindset that promotes long-term success. You can set yourself up for success as a trader by adopting a "zone" mentality, maintaining emotional detachment from the market, and focusing on the process rather than short-term outcomes. Continuous improvement, both in terms of trading knowledge and personal development, will keep you sharp, adaptive, and mentally ready for anything the market throws at you.

Trading in the zone is not an accident; it is the consequence of intentional mental conditioning, self-awareness, and discipline. As you continue to cultivate these characteristics, you will find yourself trading with greater clarity, confidence, and consistency, regardless of the market conditions

Trading in The Zone

CONCLUSION

The Ultimate Psychological Edge for Trading

The significance of establishing and mastering your mindset to succeed in trading has been a consistent topic across the pages of this book. Strategy and technical talents can get you far, but they are just part of the picture. To achieve great success, you must cultivate the psychological edge that enables you to navigate the market with discipline, clarity, and emotional detachment. This is what we mean by trading in the zone: reaching a state of mental focus and control that matches your actions with your long-term objectives.

Throughout this journey, we've covered the most important components of trading psychology, such as mental clarity, emotion management, overcoming limiting beliefs, and probabilistic thinking. In this section, we will review the important lessons and offer some concluding comments on how to continue mastering your attitude as you progress in your trading career.

Key Lessons for Consistent, Zone-based Trading.

The first and most crucial lesson is to recognize that trading is both a mental and technical game. Many traders believe that if they just learn the proper strategy or find the perfect indication, they will be able to figure out the market. However, even the best strategies will fail if your thinking is not in sync with your objectives. Developing mental discipline, staying consistent in your technique, and maintaining emotional detachment are what genuinely distinguish successful traders from those who struggle.

Staying in control of your emotions is important. Trading can cause intense sensations of fear, greed, and excitement, all of which can impair your judgment. As we described in previous chapters, these emotions can lead to harmful actions such as overtrading, revenge trading, or abandoning your goal in the heat of the moment. Learning to recognize and mitigate these emotional triggers through mindfulness, discipline, and a strong process-oriented attitude is essential for maintaining stability.

One of the most powerful tools you have is the ability to think in probabilities. Successful traders recognize that individual trades are part of a bigger process and that no one conclusion determines their success or failure. By focusing on probability and risk management, you may reduce the pressure on every single trade and approach the market more objectively. This perspective shift enables you to remain grounded and focused on the broader picture, even in the face of losses.

Finally, we've discussed the importance of beliefs and how they influence your behavior and market results. As you advance as a trader, you should frequently assess your beliefs about trading, money, and risk. Are they empowering you, or are they holding you back? Shifting limiting beliefs into positive ones can have a significant impact on your trade performance and confidence.

The Way Forward: Mastering the Art of Trading in the Zone

While this book has given you the tools to begin creating your psychological edge, the journey does not end there. Trading, like any other talent, requires ongoing development and refining. As markets evolve, so will your strategies and approach. Mastering the skill of trading in the zone is a lifetime endeavor that needs constant self-awareness, introspection, and learning.

Maintaining your psychological edge involves constantly reviewing and adjusting your trading technique. Regularly evaluate your trades to identify where you've excelled and where you may improve. This is more than just detecting faults; it's also about understanding your thought processes and how your mentality may have influenced your choices. Were there occasions when you acted in fear? Did you pursue a trade owing to overconfidence? The more you think about your psychological state when trading, the better you'll be at managing it in the future.

Continuous education is another important aspect of maintaining your success. Markets develop, as does trading knowledge. Stay sharp by learning new strategies, tools, and psychological techniques. Participate in the trading community, whether through online forums, books, or courses, to extend your perspective. The more you learn, the more you may improve your technical abilities and psychological resilience.

Don't overlook the importance of maintaining your mental and physical wellness. Trading requires a great level of concentration and discipline, and burnout can easily derail your progress. Make time for leisure, exercise, and mental health. Mindfulness and meditation can help you stay focused and emotionally balanced both within and outside of the trading room. A healthy body and mind will help you to start each trading day with new vigor and focus.

Final Thoughts on Trading Success

The path to trading success is not straightforward. There will be both happy and bad days. However, the traders that succeed in the long run are those who remain consistent in their technique, maintain emotional control, and maintain a growth-oriented mindset. They recognize that losses are a natural part of the process, and they do not let short-term failures dictate their long-term goals.

Think back on the personal stories and experiences described in this book. Each defeat taught me significant insights, not only about the markets but also about myself. Learning to accept responsibility for my trades, appreciating the value of mental clarity, and always perfecting my psychological approach have all contributed to my success. I didn't get to this level of understanding overnight; it required years of effort, introspection, and resilience. And the truth is that I'm still learning.

Trading in the zone is not about perfection; it is about being present and in control. It's all about trusting your approach, controlling your emotions, and thinking in possibilities rather than certainties. When you approach the market with this perspective, you have a significant psychological edge that helps you to confidently and clearly navigate its complexity.

I encourage you to keep moving forward, no matter where you are on your trading path. Take the principles you've learned here, put them into practice on a consistent basis, and keep improving your technical skills and mental attitude. As you have a better understanding of yourself and the markets, trading in the zone will become second nature. And once that happens, you'll be well on your way to the long-term success you've been striving for.

The Psychological Advantage for Long-Term Success

Finally, remember that your psychological edge is your most significant asset when trading. Strategies come and go, and market conditions shift, but your perspective will ultimately define your success. The ability to remain disciplined, focused, and emotionally distant distinguishes the best traders from the rest. So, continue to invest in your mental development in the same way that you would in technical expertise.

By committing to this journey, you are not only becoming a better trader but also creating a mindset that will benefit you in all aspects of your life. Trading in the zone is about mastering both yourself and the markets. Keep that in mind as you progress, and you'll discover that the benefits go far beyond financial gain.

www.ingramcontent.com/pod-product-compliance
Lightning Source LLC
Chambersburg PA
CBHW050259230526
45471CB00005B/1945